Become Who You Were Created to Be!

Teresa Velardi

Art by David Bowman, "My Child" and "Innocence" included within is printed with the artist's permission.
Artist is unknown on other drawings within the content.

Song lyrics to "Masterpiece" are the artist's and songwriters' property.
Song lyrics to "Overcomer" are the artist's and songwriters' property.

All scriptures taken from the NIV version of the Holy Bible

Layout by Ambicionz

ISBN: 978-1-955668-25-5

KINGDOM
BOOK ENDEAVORS

To all who have forgotten
who you were created to be.
Enjoy the journey as you remember.

Introduction

I believe we were all born with gifts, talents, and a purpose created by God and are here to fulfill our purpose using those gifts and talents.

The world and its happenings can easily sidetrack us from God's plan. We can easily get caught up in people, places, and things that distract us from His purpose and plan for us, especially at this time and in this place. Just look around, and you'll see the worldly ways doing their best to take us off our path to becoming who and what we were created to be.

The following pages are an invitation to step into your best life, your best ways of being, your best relationships, and all the goodness God intended for you to have. The content will remind you who you are in Christ, a child of the Most High God, creator of the entire universe! You were created in His image, and he has a plan for you.

We are all lost until we choose to look to Him instead of the worldly distractions, I know I was, and it's still easy to be distracted. Many of us are lost in toxic relationships, habits, and addictions and don't know how to break free from them. There is a way…Jesus is the Way!

I know this from my own life experience. I chose to marry a man who was not God's choice for me. I know this because I heard God tell me that he had someone so much better for me while I was standing at the altar on my wedding day. That wasn't the first poor choice I'd made, yet it was the one that took me face to face with my reflection in the mirror, asking an all-important question.

"Who are you, and why are you here?"

That was a two-fold question. Who had I become, and why was I still in my marriage? I was lost, hurting, and being hurt physically and emotionally by my then-husband. I felt far from God and needed to find out why I was even on this planet. I knew He gifted me many talents, and I wasn't using them. I felt dead inside.

My hope in putting these pages together is that you will begin your journey to becoming who you were created to be. There are some thought-provoking pages and scriptures with pages for you to record those thoughts.

My prayer for you is that you will come to know the person God created you to be. There will be both joy and sorrow along the way. So keep the tissues handy, and snuggle up close to Jesus. He will never leave you or forsake you.

With much love and many blessings,

Teresa

Daughter

This morning I asked God what He wanted me to know.

I boldly said, show me what heaven is doing, Lord. Show me what you want me to see.

My heart is open to receiving whatever you have for me right now, and this is what he said…

I wrote as the Spirit spoke to me and I felt led to share...

I see you, daughter.

I see your struggles, your tears, your pain.

I see your anxiety about this and that.

I see your inner struggle to do it all and fix it all and how you wonder how it's all going to work out.

How you feel so insignificant.

But from where I'm sitting, things look different.

You look beautiful.

You are strong.

I am proud of you.

From my everlasting throne, things are clearer.

They are already done.

I am in control.

My perspective is one of Victory and you have access to come sit up here with me.

Because of my son, you have permission to sit with me in heavenly places.

To dine at my table.

Come up here, daughter.

Come see what heaven is doing.

Come hear what I think about you.

This is your invitation anytime the world tries to steal your peace; just come up here.

Because of my son, you have permission to sit with me in heavenly places.
To dine at my table.
Come up here, daughter.
Come see what heaven is doing.
Come hear what I think about you.
This is your invitation anytime the world tries to steal your peace; just come up here.

Come crawl into my lap, for it is big enough for you and all your worries.
Fix your mind on me, and you will find perfect rest. Let me wrap you in my love, for there is no fear in love. My perfect love casts out all fear.
Every fear you have will drift away and never return while you are sitting in your papa's lap.

My embrace is all you need every time the flood of thoughts comes that try to take you under.
Let me hold you here against my heart and sing you a new song of love today.
There are so many things I want to tell you, are you listening?
There are so many things I want to show you, will you have your eyes fixed on me?

Don't allow the enemy to distract you any longer, his tactics are never new.
Yet my mercies are new every morning.

-Unknown author

8

Artist Unknown

Yet you, Lord, are our Father,
We are the clay, You are the potter;
we are all the work of Your hand.
Isaiah 64:8

Artist Unknown

Yet you, Lord, are our Father,
We are the clay, You are the potter;
we are all the work of Your hand.

Isaiah 64:8

For I know the plans I have for you," declares the Lord, "plans to prosper you and not to harm you, plans to give you hope and a future.

Jeremiah 29:11

I can do all this through him who

gives me strength.

Philippians 4:13

Jesus told him, "Don't be afraid;
just believe."
Mark 5:36

And we know that in all things
God works for the good of those who
love him, who have been called
according to his purpose.
Romans 8:28

20

Now to him who is able to do immeasurably more than all we ask or imagine, according to his power that is at work within us, to him be glory in the church and in Christ Jesus throughout all generations, for ever and ever! Amen.
Ephesians 3:20-21

Fight the good fight of the faith.
Take hold of the eternal life to
which you were called when you
made your good confession in the
presence of many witnesses.
1 Timothy 6:12

Finally, brothers and sisters,
whatever is true, whatever is noble,
whatever is right, whatever is pure,
whatever is lovely, whatever is admirable
—if anything is excellent or
praiseworthy—think about such things.
Philippians 4:8

*Trust in the Lord with all your
heart and lean not on your own understanding;
in all your ways submit to him,
and he will make your paths straight.
Proverbs 3: 5-6*

But the fruit of the Spirit is love,
joy, peace, forbearance, kindness,
goodness, faithfulness, gentleness
and self-control. Against such things
there is no law.
Galatians 5:22-23

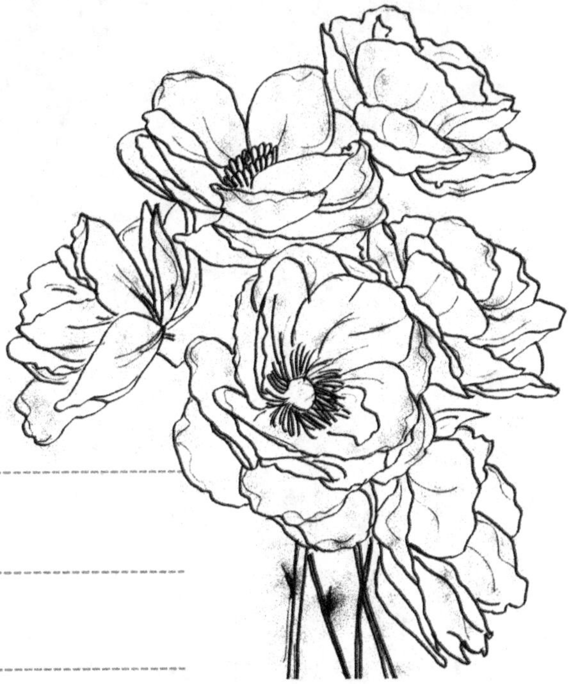

Innocence - Artist, David Bowman

Jesus Christ is the same yesterday
and today and forever.
Hebrews 13:8

Ask and it will be given to you; seek
and you will find; knock and the door
will be opened to you.
Matthew 7:7

For it is by grace you have been saved, through faith—and this is not from yourselves, it is the gift of God— not by works, so that no one can boast.

Ephesians 2:8-9

Therefore, since we are surrounded by such a great cloud of witnesses, let us throw off everything that hinders and the sin that so easily entangles. And let us run with perseverance the race marked out for us, fixing our eyes on Jesus, the pioneer and perfecter of faith. For the joy set before him he endured the cross, scorning its shame, and sat down at the right hand of the throne of God.
Hebrew 12:1-2

Do not conform to the pattern of this world,
but be transformed by the renewing of your
mind. Then you will be able to test and
approve what God's will is—his good,
pleasing and perfect will.
Romans 12:2

The Armor of God

Ephesians 6:10-18

10 Finally, be strong in the Lord and in his mighty power.

11 Put on the full armor of God, so that you can take your stand against the devil's schemes.

12 For our struggle is not against flesh and blood, but against the rulers, against the authorities, against the powers of this dark world and against the spiritual forces of evil in the heavenly realms.

13 Therefore put on the full armor of God, so that when the day of evil comes, you may

14 be able to stand your ground, and after you have done everything, to stand.

15 Stand firm then, with the belt of truth buckled around your waist, with the breastplate of righteousness in place,

16 and with your feet fitted with the readiness that comes from the gospel of peace.

17 In addition to all this, take up the shield of faith, with which you can extinguish all the flaming arrows of the evil one.

18 Take the helmet of salvation and the sword of the Spirit, which is the word of God.

And pray in the Spirit on all occasions with all kinds of prayers and requests. With this in mind, be alert and always keep on praying for all the Lord's people.

For the Lord is good and his
love endures forever;
his faithfulness continues through
all generations.
Psalm 100:5

Let the message of Christ dwell among you richly as you teach and admonish one another with all wisdom through psalms, hymns, and songs from the Spirit, singing to God with gratitude in your hearts.

Colossians 3:16

A friend loves at all times.

Proverbs 17:17

Blessed are the pure of heart for
they shall see God.
Matthew 5:8

With God all things are possible.
Matthew 19:2

My Child - Artist, David Bowman

Give thanks to the Lord, for
he is good;
his love endures forever.
Psalm 107:1

12 Yet to all who did receive him, to those who believed in his name, he gave the right to become children of God— 13 children born not of natural descent, nor of human decision or a husband's will, but born of God.

John 1:12-13

His divine power has given us everything we need for a godly life through our knowledge of him who called us by his own glory and goodness.

2 Peter 1:3

If God is for us, who can ever be against us?

Romans 8:31

For God so loved the world that he gave his one and only Son, that whoever believes in him shall not perish but have eternal life.

John 3:16

Psalm 91

1 Whoever dwells in the shelter of the Most High will rest in the shadow of the Almighty.

2 I will say of the Lord, "He is my refuge and my fortress, my God, in whom I trust."

3 Surely he will save you from the fowler's snare and from the deadly pestilence.

4 He will cover you with his feathers, and under his wings you will find refuge; his faithfulness will be your shield and rampart.

5 You will not fear the terror of night, nor the arrow that flies by day,

6 nor the pestilence that stalks in the darkness, nor the plague that destroys at midday.

7 A thousand may fall at your side, ten thousand at your right hand, but it will not come near you.

8 You will only observe with your eyes and see the punishment of the wicked.

9 If you say, "The Lord is my refuge," and you make the Most High your dwelling,

10 no harm will overtake you, no disaster will come near your tent.

11 For he will command his angels concerning you to guard you in all your ways;

12 they will lift you up in their hands, so that you will not strike your foot against a stone.

Psalm 91

13 You will tread on the lion and the cobra; you will trample the great lion and the serpent.

14 "Because he loves me," says the Lord, "I will rescue him; I will protect him, for he acknowledges my name.

15 He will call on me, and I will answer him; I will be with him in trouble, I will deliver him and honor him.

16 With long life I will satisfy him and show him my salvation."

As the Father has loved me, so have I loved you. Now remain in my love. If you keep my commands, you will remain in my love, just as I have kept my Father's commands and remain in his love.

John 15:9-10

Lord, you are my God;
I will exalt you and praise your name,
for in perfect faithfulness
you have done wonderful things,
things planned long ago.
Isaiah 25:1

If the Son sets you free, you will be free indeed.

John 8:36

In Him we have redemption through his blood, the forgiveness of sins, in accordance with the riches of God's grace.

Ephesians 1:7

Jesus replied: "'Love the Lord your God with all your heart and with all your soul and with all your mind.' This is the first and greatest commandment. And the second is like it: 'Love your neighbor as yourself.'"
Matthew 22:37-39

From the Desk of God

Effective Immediately:

Please be aware that you need to make changes in your life. These changes need to be completed so that I may fulfill my promises to you to grant you peace, joy, and happiness in this life. I apologize for any inconvenience; this seems very little to ask of you after all I am doing. I know. I already gave you the 10 Commandments. Keep them. But follow these guidelines as well.

Quit Worrying

Life has dealt you a blow, and all you do is sit and worry. Have you forgotten that I am here to take all of your burdens and carry them for you? Or do you enjoy fretting over every little thing that comes your way?

Put it on the List

Something needs to be done or taken care of. Put it on the list. No, not YOUR list. Put it on MY to-do list. Let ME be the one to take care of the problem. I can't help you until you turn it over to me. And, although my to-do list is long, I am, after all, God. I can take care of anything you put into my hands. In fact, if the truth were ever really known, I take care of many things for you that you never even realize.

Trust Me

Once you've given your burdens to Me, quit trying to take them back. Trust in me. Have the faith that I will take care of all your needs, problems, and trials. Problems with the kids? Put them on my list. Problem with finances? Put it on my list. Problems with your emotional roller coaster? For my sake, put it on my list. I want to help you. All you have to do is ask.

Leave it Alone

Don't wake up one morning and say, "Well, I'm feeling much stronger now; I think I can handle it from here." Why do you think you are feeling stronger now? It's simple. You gave me your burdens, and I'm taking care of them. I also renew your strength and cover you in my peace. Don't you know that you will be right back where you started if I give you these problems back? Leave them with me and forget about them. Just let me do my job.

Talk to Me

I want you to forget a lot of things. Forget what was making you crazy. Forget the worry and fretting because you know I'm in control. But there's one thing I pray you never forget. Please don't forget to talk to me – OFTEN! I love you. I want to hear your voice. I want you to include me in the things going on in your life. I want to listen to you talk about your friends and family. Prayer is simply you having a conversation with me. I want to be your dearest friend.

Have Faith

I see many things from up here that you can't see from where you are. Have faith in me that I know what I'm doing. Trust me; you wouldn't want the view from my eyes. I will continue to care for you, watch over you and meet your needs. You only have to trust me. Although I have a much bigger task than you, it seems as if you have so much trouble just doing your simple part. How hard can trust be?

Share

You were taught to share when you were only two years old. When did you forget? That rule still applies. Share with those who are less fortunate than you. Share your joy with those who need encouragement. Share your laughter with those who haven't heard any in such a long time. Share your tears with those who have forgotten how to cry. Share your faith with those who have none.

Be Patient

I managed to fix it so you could have so many diverse experiences in just one lifetime. You grow from a child to an adult, have children, change jobs many times, learn many trades, travel to many places, meet thousands of people, and experience so much. How can you be so impatient then when it takes Me a little longer than you expect to handle something on my to-do list? Trust in My timing, for My timing is perfect. Just because I created the entire universe in only six days, everyone thinks I should always rush, rush, rush.

Be Kind

Be kind to others, for I love them just as much as I love you. They may not dress like you, talk like you, or live the same way you do, but I still love you all. Please try to get along, for my sake. I created each of you differently in some way. It would be too boring if you were all identical. Please know I love each of your differences.

Love Yourself

As much as I love you, how can you not love yourself? You were created by me for one reason only – to be loved and to love in return. I am a God of Love. Love me. Love your neighbors. But also love yourself. It makes my heart ache when I see you so angry with yourself when things go wrong. You are very precious to me. Don't ever forget that!

With all my heart, I love you,
GOD ♥

Author Unknown

You will seek me and find me when you seek me with all your heart.

Jeremiah 29:13

But you are a chosen people, a royal priesthood, a holy nation, God's special possession, that you may declare the praises of him who called you out of darkness into his wonderful light.

1 Peter 2:9

Truly, I say to you, unless you
turn and become like children, you will
never enter the kingdom of heaven.
Matthew 18:3

When anxiety was great within me,
your consolation brought me joy.
Psalm 94:19

For the word of God is alive and active. Sharper than any double-edged sword, it penetrates even to dividing soul and spirit, joints and marrow; it judges the thoughts and attitudes of the heart.

Hebrews 4:12

The Power of "I Am"

Teresa Velardi

God Said to Moses, "I AM that I AM"
Exodus 3:14

*"Whatever follows 'I AM' will
come looking for you."*
Joel Osteen

Did you know that every word you speak has power? Yes! Every word, especially "I AM" statements. The Holy Spirit lives within us. The God who created the universe resides in our hearts. Every time you say, "I AM," you invoke the power of the Holy Spirit. Before making that "I AM" statement, make sure you are willing to receive what follows those powerful words!

I AM Blessed

I AM Gifted

I AM Talented

I AM Thoughtful

I AM Kind

I AM Forgiving

I AM Grateful

I AM Beautiful

I AM Fearless

I AM a Child of God

I AM Strong

I AM Courageous

I AM Inspired

I AM Enough

I AM Patient

I AM Adventurous

I AM Loved

I AM Generous

I AM Successful

I AM Anointed

I AM Healthy

I AM Victorious

I AM Confident

I AM Well-Able

I AM Fabulous

I AM Highly Favored

I AM Determined

I AM Compassionate

I AM Loving

I AM Fun

I AM Brave

I AM Abundant

Now it's your turn. How many "I AM Statements can you make about yourself?

I AM _____   I AM _____

I AM _____   I AM _____

I AM _____   I AM _____

I AM _____   I AM _____

I AM _____   I AM _____

I AM _____   I AM _____

I AM _____   I AM _____

I AM _____   I AM _____

I AM _____   I AM _____

I AM _____   I AM _____

I AM _____   I AM _____

I AM _____   I AM _____

I AM _____   I AM _____

I AM _____   I AM _____

I AM _____   I AM _____

I AM _____   I AM _____

I AM _____   I AM _____

I AM _____   I AM _____

I AM _____   I AM _____

I AM _____   I AM _____

And let the peace of Christ rule in your hearts, to which indeed you were called in one body. And be thankful.
Colossians 3:15

Shout for joy to the Lord, all the earth. Worship the Lord with gladness; come before him with joyful songs. Know that the Lord is God.

Psalm 100:1

Give thanks in all circumstances; for this is God's will for you in Christ Jesus.
1 Thessalonians 5:18

Oh give thanks to the Lord, for he is good, for his steadfast love endures forever!
Psalm 107:1

Be strong and courageous. Do not be afraid or terrified because of them, for the Lord your God goes with you; he will never leave you nor forsake you."

Deuteronomy 31:6

Live with a Grateful Heart

Teresa Velardi

And he directed the people to sit down on the grass. Taking the five loaves and the two fish and looking up to heaven, he gave thanks and broke the loaves. Then he gave them to the disciples, and the disciples gave them to the people. They all ate and were satisfied, and the disciples picked up twelve basketfuls of broken pieces that were left over.The number of those who ate was about five thousand men, besides women and children.

Matthew 14:19-22

This scripture is the most beautiful example of the power of gratitude I can find anywhere. When Jesus was teaching the people, and they became hungry, instead of sending them out to find food on their own, He instructed His disciples to feed the people.

When all they could find in the crowd was a little boy's lunch of five small loaves and two fish, they brought them to Jesus, wondering how this would feed so many.

What does the scripture say Jesus did? He looked up to heaven and gave thanks. The food multiplied exponentially and fed all the people on that hillside with twelve baskets left after everyone had eaten. He gave thanks!

Gratitude is the key to an abundant life.

How would your life be different if you lived with a grateful heart? If you are thankful for everything, every situation, good and not so good? When it comes to the "not so good," let's pause for a minute. Did you get through it? Is your life better because you did? Did you end up being grateful for whatever that situation was? My guess is you answered, "Yes." God knows what we need.

"With man, this is impossible, but with God, ALL things are possible."
Matthew 19:26

God wants to give us the desires of our hearts, our grateful hearts! That's only one reason why a daily gratitude practice is essential.

Gratitude for the people in your life, what you have, who you are, and who you value essentially says, "I would like to have more of this, more of these kinds of people in my life."

Do you have a daily gratitude practice? What are you grateful for? Who? Are you praying for something in your life to change? Find gratitude in that situation, ask God to help you through it, and find the life-changing lesson.

Many people in the "self-help" world advocate for having a daily gratitude practice. One of them is the late Bob Proctor, who also taught people to be grateful for what is potentially in their future. If you are working toward a goal in your life, see it as already reached, and be thankful. His gratitude statement is:

"I'm so happy and grateful now that_____." You fill in the blank.

One of my very good friends created a website with a story relative to her life. Whether she was "rich" or "poor," her life was always abundant. You can read her story "Two Fishes" at: https://bit.ly/Two_Fishes

What's on your gratitude list today? Write at least three people, places, or things you are grateful for on the next page. If you want to share it and encourage others to do the same, I invite you to join my Grateful Hearts Community on Facebook and post there. http://bit.ly/Grateful-Hearts

This is the day that the Lord has made; let us rejoice and be glad in it.

Psalms 118:24

Rejoice always, pray without
ceasing, give thanks in all
circumstances; for this is the will of
God in Christ Jesus for you.
Thessalonians 5:16-18

May God himself, the God of peace, sanctify you through and through. May your whole spirit, soul and body be kept blameless at the coming of our Lord Jesus Christ. The one who calls you is faithful, and he will do it.

1 Thessalonians 5:23-24

Cast all your anxiety on him because

he cares for you.

1 Peter 5:7

For the word of God is alive and active. Sharper than any double-edged sword, it penetrates even to dividing soul and spirit, joints and marrow; it judges the thoughts and attitudes of the heart.

Hebrews 4:12

But thanks be to God, who in Christ always leads us in triumphal procession, and through us spreads the fragrance of the knowledge of him everywhere.
2 Corinthians 2:14

Now you are the body of Christ, and each one of you is a part of it. And God has placed in the church first of all apostles, second prophets, third teachers, then miracles, then gifts of healing, of helping, of guidance, and of different kinds of tongues.
1 Corinthians 27-28

For where your treasure is, there
your heart will be also.
Matthew 6:21

Count it all joy, my brothers, when you meet trials of various kinds, for you know that the testing of your faith produces steadfastness. And let steadfastness have its full effect, that you may be perfect and complete, lacking in nothing.

James 1:2-4

Bless the Lord, O my soul, and forget not all his benefits, who forgives all your iniquity, who heals all your diseases, who redeems your life from the pit, who crowns you with steadfast love and mercy, who satisfies you with good so that your youth is renewed like the eagle's.

Psalm 103:2-5

Metamorphosis

You are a butterfly in the making!
Teresa Velardi

That little hungry caterpillar attaches itself to the limb of its favorite tree.

It then wraps itself into a malleable shell called a cocoon.

Waiting in the darkness, that little caterpillar is transforming.

When the time is right, it struggles to break out of the darkness of the cocoon. Its wings are formed and need to be strengthened in the process.

Now a butterfly, it stretches its wings and flies free!

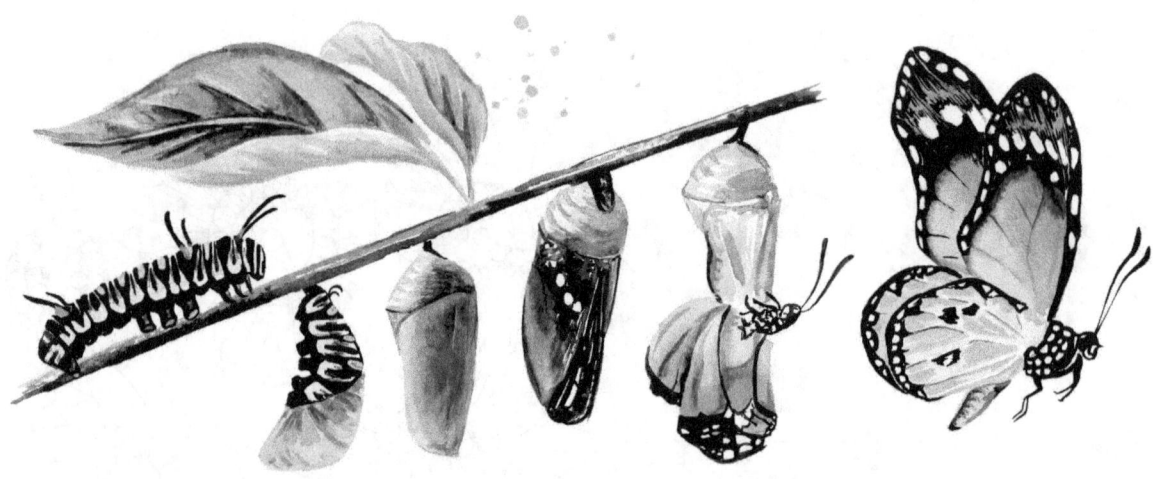

Let us acknowledge the Lord;
let us press on to acknowledge him.
As surely as the sun rises,
he will appear;
he will come to us like the winter rains,
like the spring rains that water the earth.
Hosea 6:3

It is for freedom that Christ has set us free. Stand firm, then, and do not let yourselves be burdened again by a yoke of slavery.
Galatians 5:1

I can do all this through him who

gives me strength.

Philippians 4:13

Jesus told him, "Don't be afraid;

just believe."

Mark 5:36

And we know that in all things
God works for the good of those who
love him, who have been called
according to his purpose.
Romans 8:28

From a Ball of Clay to a Work of Art
A Journey Through the Potter's Hands

Teresa Velardi

Have you ever wondered how that beautiful piece of pottery came to be on the shelf in the gallery?

It's a process, sometimes painful, especially when you think about it as an illustration of life.

God is the Potter, and we are the Clay

There are many steps to be made in the process.

- **Prepare the clay** – This is called wedging and is like kneading stiff dough. Wedging removes any air bubbles in the clay as it gets pounded, pushed, twisted, and manipulated into a ball that will go onto the potter's wheel. The clay must be made ready for its transformational journey from a ball of clay to a work of art.

- **Center** – The clay gets forcefully dropped onto the wheel so it will stick. Then, while the wheel is spinning very fast, the potter pushes the clay toward the center of the wheel. It is centered when there is no "wobble" in the clay. It feels smooth and almost looks like it's still when perfectly centered.

- **Open** – After centering, with the wheel still spinning very fast, the potter opens a hole in the center of the clay. Using both hands, the potter moves the clay outwardly to define the inside and outside, preparing for the next step.

- **Mold and Shape** – With one hand inside and the other outside, the potter "pulls" the clay upward, pushing with fingers both inside and outside, causing the clay to grow taller or wider, molding and shaping the clay into the desired vessel shape. Once shaped to the potter's satisfaction, the piece is set aside to dry slightly.

- **Trim** – The piece is turned upside down and re-centered on the wheel to trim excess clay at the bottom. While the wheel turns, the potter uses sharp tools to trim away whatever is seen as excess. With the trimming completed, and any design elements gently carved into the leather like clay, the potter marks the piece with an identifying symbol or signature and sets it aside to dry thoroughly.

- **Into the fire** – Once completely dry, pieces are placed into the kiln to be "fired." The impurities are burned out of the clay, and the pottery is made strong during exposure to extreme heat. Once the kiln cools, the pieces are moved to the next step.

- **Glazing** – The pot is dusted off after the firing, and the potter now has a "blank canvas" to add color and design. A glaze is a scientifically formulated mixture of elements and pigments from the earth that bring color to the work once it goes through the second firing. Glaze can be applied by dipping, brushing, spattering, and many other ways, depending on the look the potter wishes to achieve. Each piece is unique and carefully thought out, just like you!

- **Into the fire** – Yes, again! Once the glaze has dried, it's time to go back into the kiln. This time it's even hotter than the first. The glaze fuses with the pot, and the heat creates a chemical reaction causing the color to come alive during the firing and creating the finished look. I call this the "beautification" fire.

- **It's showtime!** Many times, potters will show their work in galleries. It's a special event when people gather to look at beautiful art.

So there you have it, the ball of clay, with the touch of the potter's hands, has become a beautiful work of art.

This process is also a metaphor for our lives. Some of us are in the kiln, screaming, "Let me out of here; it's too hot!" Others are spinning around, not knowing where they are, what to do, or how to stop what's happening.

While we wonder how to stop the spinning or get out of the fire, God is there. He's the potter. He watches over us through every step of our lives, even when we think He's absent. We've got to trust Him. Every decision we make affects our lives. Trying times, provided that we face and endure them, rather than running away, build character and make us stronger, better people.

God has a reason for creating you, and He has a plan for your life.

"For I know the plans I have for you," declares the Lord, "plans to prosper you and not to harm you, plans to give you hope and a future."
Jeremiah 29:11

He's also there with us when we are in the fire. He was in the fire with Shadrach, Meshach, and Abednego in the book of Daniel. (Daniel 3:16-28) He wants us to seek Him and trust Him.

Draw close to God, for He is the potter, and we absent. We've got to trust Him. Every decision we make affects our lives. Trying times, provided that we face and endure them, rather than running away, build character and make us stronger, better people.

Yet you, Lord, are our Father,
We are the clay, You are the potter;
we are all the work of Your hand.

Isaiah 64:8

145

*For the Lord is good and his
love endures forever;
his faithfulness continues through
all generations.
Psalm 100:5*

Blessed are the pure of heart for
they shall see God.
Matthew 5:8

Jesus Christ is the same yesterday
and today and forever.
Hebrews 13:8

Do not conform to the pattern of this world, but be transformed by the renewing of your mind. Then you will be able to test and approve what God's will is—his good, pleasing and perfect will.

Romans 12:2

Masterpiece

Danny Gokey

Heartbreak's a bittersweet sound
Know it well
It's ringing in my ears
And I can't understand
Why I'm not fixed by now
Begged and I pleaded
Take this pain but I'm still bleeding

Heart trusts you for certain
Head says it's not working
I'm stuck here still hurting
But you tell me

You're making a masterpiece
You shaping the soul in me
You're moving where I can't see
And all I am is in your hands
You're taking me all apart
Like it was your plan from the start
To finish your work of art for all to see you're making a masterpiece

Guess I'm your canvas
Beautiful black and blue
Painted in mercy's hue
I don't see past this
But you see me now
Who I'll be then
There at the end
Standing there as

Your Masterpiece
You're shaping the soul in me
You're moving where I can't see
And all I am is in your hands
You're taking me all apart
Like it was your plan from the start
To finish your work of art for all to see
You're making a masterpiece
You're making a masterpiece

Even though I'm hurting
I'll let you keep working
You're making a masterpiece
You're shaping the soul in me
You're moving where I can't see
And all I am is in your hands

You're taking me all apart
Like it was your plan from the start
To finish your work of art for all to see you're making a masterpiece
You're making a masterpiece
I'll be your masterpiece

Songwriters: Bernie Herms, Emily Weisband

For we are God's handiwork, created in Christ Jesus to do good works, which God prepared in advance for us to do.

Ephesians 2:10

157

Finally, brothers and sisters, whatever is true,
whatever is noble, whatever is right, whatever is
pure, whatever is lovely, whatever is admirable
—if anything is excellent or praiseworthy—
think about such things.
Philippians 4:8

Ask and it will be given to you; seek and you will find; knock and the door will be opened to you.

Matthew 7:7

For the Lord is good and his love
endures forever;
his faithfulness continues through
all generations.
Psalm 100:5

Let the message of Christ dwell among you richly as you teach and admonish one another with all wisdom through psalms, hymns, and songs from the Spirit, singing to God with gratitude in your hearts.

Colossians 3:16

Overcomer

Mandisa

Staring at a stop sign
Watching people drive by
T. Mac on the radio
Got so much on your mind
Nothing's really going right
Looking for a ray of hope

Whatever it is you may be going through
I know He's not gonna let it get the best of you

You're an overcomer
Stay in the fight until the final round
You're not going under
"Cause God is holding you right now
You might be down for a moment
Feeling like it's hopeless
That's when He reminds You
That you're an overcomer
You're an overcomer

Everybody's been down
Hit the bottom, hit the ground
Oh, you're not alone
Just take a breath, don't forget
Hang on to His promises
He wants You to know

You're an overcomer
Stay in the fight until the final round
You're not going under
'Cause God is holding you right now

You might be down for a moment
Feeling like it's hopeless
That's when He reminds You
That you're an overcomer
You're an overcomer

The same Man, the Great I am
The one who overcame death
Is living inside of You
So just hold tight, fix your eyes
On the one who holds your life
There's nothing he can't do
He's telling you

You're an overcomer
Stay in the fight until the final round
You're not going under
 'Cause God is holding you right now
You might be down for a moment
Feeling like it's hopeless
That's when He reminds You
That you're an overcomer
You're an overcomer
You're an overcomer
You're an overcomer

So don't quit, don't give in
You're an overcomer
Don't quit, don't give in
You're an overcomer
Don't quit, don't give in
You're an overcomer
You're an overcomer

Songwriters: David Arthur Garcia, Benjamin Glover, Christopher E Stevens

Fight the good fight of the faith. Take hold of the eternal life to which you were called when you made your good confession in the presence of many witnesses.
1 Timothy 6:12

Now to him who is able to do immeasurably more than all we ask or imagine, according to his power that is at work within us, to him be glory in the church and in Christ Jesus throughout all generations, for ever and ever! Amen.

Ephesians 3:20-21

The Spirit of the Sovereign Lord is
on me, because the Lord has anointed me
to proclaim good news to the poor. He
has sent me to bind up the brokenhearted,
to proclaim freedom for the captives and
release from darkness for the prisoners.
Isaiah 61:1

"I have told you these things, so that in me you may have peace. In this world you will have trouble. But take heart! I have overcome the world."

John 16:33

And we know that in all things
God works for the good of those who
love him, who have been called
according to his purpose.
Romans 8:28

Broken Toys

Ben Hildner

As children bring their broken toys, with tears, for me to mend

I brought my broken dreams to God because he was my friend.

But then, instead of leaving Him in peace to work alone
I hung around and tried to help . . . with ways that were my own.

At last I snatched them back and cried, "How can You be so slow?"

"My child," He said. "What could I do? You never did let go.

Yet you, Lord, are our Father,
We are the clay, You are the potter;
we are all the work of Your hand.

Isaiah 64:8

For I know the plans I have for you," declares the Lord, "plans to prosper you and not to harm you, plans to give you hope and a future.

Jeremiah 29:11

I can do all this through him who

gives me strength.

Philippians 4:13

Jesus told him, "Don't be afraid;
just believe."
Mark 5:36

We love because he first loved us.

1 John 4:19